SIMPLY
piano

Robyn Payne

HB

HINKLER
BOOKS

Many thanks to Neil Payne for endless reading of manuscripts
and to Louise Coulthard for her patience

Published by Hinkler Books Pty Ltd
45–55 Fairchild Street
Heatherton Victoria 3202 Australia
www.hinklerbooks.com

Author: Robyn Payne
Project manager and editor: Louise Coulthard
Book cover design: Sam Grimmer and Mandi Cole
Photography: Ned Meldrum
Prepress: Graphic Print Group

ISBN: 978 1 7418 5476 3

Printed and bound in China

CONTENTS

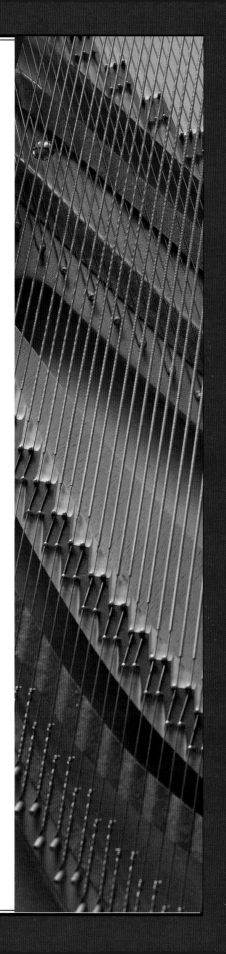

INTRODUCTION 4

CHOOSING A PIANO 5

PARTS OF THE PIANO 6

CARING FOR THE PIANO 8

POSTURE AND HAND POSITION 10

TO READ OR NOT TO READ 11

RECOGNISING THE KEYS 12

LET'S PLAY STRAIGHT AWAY 14

LEARNING SCALES AND
LISTENING 20

READING MUSIC MADE EASY I 26

READING MUSIC MADE EASY II 32

EXERCISES FOR FINGER
INDEPENDENCE 36

PLAY SOME POPULAR CLASSICS 40

PRACTICE TECHNIQUE 45

ACCOMPANIMENT USING BASS
AND CHORDS 46

BOOGIE PIANO 50

USING THE PEDALS 57

CHORD PROGRESSIONS 58

IMPROVISATION: SCALES 70

IMPROVISATION: CHORDS AND
MELODIES 74

TWO NEW CHORDS 77

CONCLUSION 79

ABOUT THE AUTHOR 80

INTRODUCTION

The piano is a percussion instrument. The musician doesn't hit anything though: the hammers hit the strings. It's one of the most versatile instruments, as it can play just about any style of music as a solo instrument, as an accompanying instrument or as part of an orchestra. The piano can also play solo versions of orchestral scores, as it covers the entire musical range of the orchestra.

The piano was a major breakthrough in the development of keyboard instruments because it plays notes softly or loudly. The full name for the piano is 'pianoforte' (in Italian, 'piano' means 'soft' and 'forte' means 'loud').

We will look at using the piano as a solo and an accompanying instrument, how to improvise and a lot more. Be patient as you work through the basics in the earlier sections. It's important to cover it all so you can keep building on your knowledge ... you need to walk before you can run!

You have taken the first important step in learning to play. The next very important step is to regularly practise what you learn. You won't miraculously learn to play the piano simply by following these lessons, but I hope you will be inspired to put in the time practising after what you've learnt.

If you find a section that you wish to learn more about, go for it! There's a wealth of information available in books, on the internet and from teachers so you can further your knowledge.

CHOOSING A PIANO

There are several types of pianos to choose from. You need to decide on an acoustic or electronic piano. Your choice may depend on issues such as budget and noise considerations, as well feel, sound and personal appeal. Space is often an issue; many people only have room for an upright or electronic piano.

ELECTRONIC PIANOS

If neighbours or family will be troubled by your constant practice, it may be best to choose an electronic piano, as they have a volume control and can connect to headphones. However, some upright acoustic pianos have a practice pedal, which greatly reduces the volume.

Electronic pianos can also connect to a computer to record your playing. Many electronic pianos already have the ability to record built in, as well as a metronome and extra sounds like organs, harpsichords and other electronic piano effects. They also need less maintenance and don't need to be tuned.

ACOUSTIC PIANOS

If you can't decide between an electronic and an acoustic piano, choose an acoustic one. There's something quite lovely about acoustic instruments and the best thing is how nice it feels when you play one. Electronic keyboards try to emulate the feel of acoustic pianos with a weighted keyboard (or action). However, nothing beats an acoustic piano for feel.

Choose a grand piano if you have room and budget permits. There's nothing nicer than the sound of the piano coming straight up at you. The action is simpler on a grand and it usually has a nicer feel than an upright piano. Grands can vary in price as much as uprights, so if you take your time, you'll be sure to find one that fits your budget.

When you've decided on which type of piano to buy, go to a piano shop or two and talk to the staff. It will be a pleasant experience learning about the instrument you're about to spend many enjoyable hours with.

Finally, before buying an acoustic piano, ask a piano tuner to look at the one you are thinking of buying. They will be able to see if you are buying any problems and if you're getting value for money.

PARTS OF THE PIANO

The piano is a mechanical marvel! Here are some of the parts that make it work.

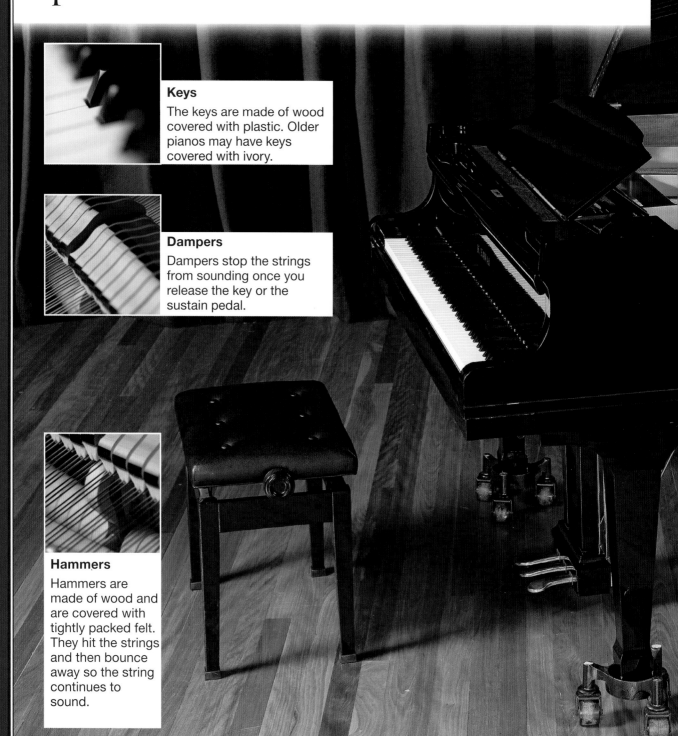

Keys

The keys are made of wood covered with plastic. Older pianos may have keys covered with ivory.

Dampers

Dampers stop the strings from sounding once you release the key or the sustain pedal.

Hammers

Hammers are made of wood and are covered with tightly packed felt. They hit the strings and then bounce away so the string continues to sound.

Lid
Open the lid when playing to give the piano a bigger and louder sound.

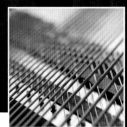

Strings
These are mainly grouped in threes and pairs and produce the sound when hit. Try not to touch them as they will rust, affecting their sound.

Tuning pins
These hold the strings to the body of the piano and alter their pitch when tuning.

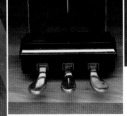

Pedals
The right pedal is the sustain pedal (not the loud pedal – there is no such thing on a piano). It lifts all the dampers off the strings together. This is the most frequently used pedal.

The left pedal is the soft or una corda pedal. On a grand piano, it moves the whole action of the piano slightly to one side, aligning the hammers with only one string (hence the name una corda – 'one string'). On an upright piano, it moves all the hammers closer to the strings, reducing the throw of the hammer and hitting the strings more softly.

Some pianos have a middle pedal. If it's a grand piano, the middle pedal is the sostenuto pedal, which is a special kind of sustain pedal. On an upright piano, it is usually a practice pedal with a locking mechanism. It lowers a felt strip over where the hammers hit the strings, making the piano play very softly – handy for late night practice or when your dedication to practice becomes wearying for others!

CARING FOR THE PIANO

With just a little care, you will have years of joy from an acoustic piano.

- An acoustic piano is mostly made of wood with an iron frame holding the strings in place. Wood is susceptible to moisture and temperature, so if you maintain a constant temperature and humidity level around the piano, the happier it will be. Varying levels of temperature and humidity can cause hammers and dampers to stick and the piano will go out of tune more often.

- Avoid putting the piano where there are draughts, vents or direct sunlight. Also avoid sitting an upright against an exterior wall that gets a lot of sun, as this can create large temperature variations. It is best to put an upright against an inside wall.

- Keep a grand piano closed when it's not being used. This helps keep dust and moisture away from the strings and will keep the piano sounding nicer for longer. Grands that have been left open for a long time can sound a bit 'honky tonk', as the strings may rust and lose their sparkle. Keeping a piano closed helps preserve everything inside, such as the strings, dampers, hammers and the moving parts.

- Have your piano tuned at least once a year, whether you think it needs it or not. The piano may sound in tune, however the pitch of the piano as a whole may drop slightly. If a piano is left like this over a few years, it becomes difficult to bring it back up to pitch. The tone suffers and it is also harder to play along with other tuned instruments.

- Clean the wooden cabinet of the piano with a clean, damp, lint-free cotton cloth. Make sure it's damp, as this stops any dust on the piano acting as an abrasive and scratching the surface.

- Pianos don't like to be stored away or rarely played – the best thing you can do for a piano is to play it regularly.

POSTURE AND HAND POSITION

POSTURE

If possible, choose a stool with an adjustable height. Set it so that your forearms are roughly parallel to the floor when your hands are resting on the keyboard. Your elbows should be slightly higher than the keys. It's important to keep the shoulders relaxed and the feet flat on the floor.

Never shrug or stoop while playing – this causes tension in the arms and neck. The idea is to keep your body as relaxed as possible and your arms loose. When I learned the correct posture, I found that I could actually get rid of a headache by playing the piano!

HAND POSITION

To establish the correct hand position:

1 Hold your hand with the palm facing up, as though you are holding an orange.

2 Turn your hand over and place it on the keys with fingers still gently curved. Fingers are never straight on the piano keyboard.

3 Keep the wrist in line with the forearm. Try not to bend it up or down. Again, keeping everything gently aligned will ensure a relaxed arm, hand and fingers.

4 Relax your shoulders. Imagine weight is falling from the shoulders straight down the arms to the wrists, so the arms stay loose.

As you progress, you will need to keep hand and finger movement to a minimum. When initially practising finger exercises, however, overemphasise finger movement to build accuracy on the keys and strengthen the fingers, hands and forearms.

Fingernails must be trimmed short, otherwise they will click on the keys and force you to play with straightened fingers, which is poor technique.

TO READ OR NOT TO READ

People may claim they can't read music nor learn to read it. My response is that learning to read music is not really important – it all depends on what you want to do with your piano playing.

Some teachers may emphasise the need to read music, however it's not necessary for learning to play and it's a shame to put this pressure on yourself. Most musicians have a tendency to be either a strong reader or have a strong ear (but you can be very good at both after practice). I will teach you to both read and develop your ear.

Reading and playing by ear are both very useful skills. I have had particular success in my career as a result of my good ear. Reading is a big asset, however. You learn so many things from reading words on a printed page: this is true with music as well. There are times when it's a joy just to open a book of piano music and play something you've never played before.

Once you know how you want to use your piano, either by accompanying yourself singing and writing songs or playing music by other composers, you can then decide how much time you choose to put into reading practice.

RECOGNISING THE KEYS

When you look at the piano keyboard for the first time, all those keys may seem a little overwhelming. How do you know which key is which? It's easy to break down the piano keyboard into smaller parts.

BLACK KEYS

When you look at the keys, you'll see that the black keys are grouped alternately in twos and threes.

Starting with the black key at the left of a group of three, play the five black notes in order. They have a particularly Oriental musical sound to them. If you hold down the right (sustain) pedal and run your finger up along the keys, it will have a harp-like sound.

Notice how low sounds are to the left and high sounds are to the right side of the keyboard.

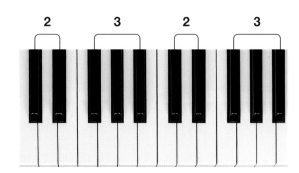

WHITE KEYS

Now find the white key to the left of a group of two black keys. This is called **C**. The white keys are named using the first seven letters of the alphabet: A, B, C, D, E, F and G.

Look at the keyboard and find all the Cs there. If you play just the white notes in order from one C to the next, you have played a C major scale. If you play these keys from left to right (or low to high), the notes are C, D, E, F, G, A, B and C. The distance from one C to the next is called an **octave**.

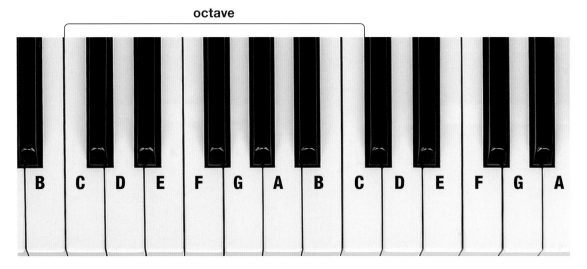

The Octave

The Western Scale (the type of tuning used on pianos and in most orchestras, rather than the tuning used in Eastern music) divides the octave into twelve equal parts called **semitones**. Count the black and white keys between one C and the next. You'll find there are twelve notes (not including the second C). The keyboard is these same twelve notes repeated over and over.

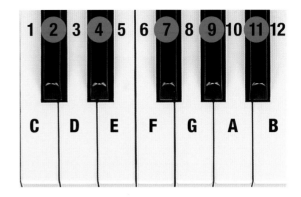

Sharps and Flats

Look at the keyboard and find every D, every G, every B and so on for all the seven letter names. Note that in each octave, there is one group of two black notes and one group of three. The words **sharp** (symbolised by #) and **flat** (symbolised by ♭) are used to name the black notes.

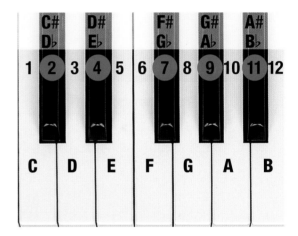

Middle C

Now find the C right in the middle of the keyboard. This is called **middle C**. This is the reference note that all pitches refer to. With your right hand, place your thumb on middle C, then rest your other fingers on the next four white notes to the right of middle C. Keep the fingers lightly curved.

Your fingers are covering C, D, E, F and G. Keeping your fingers only on these keys, play up and down the notes. Try doing this in other positions on the piano: you will first have to find the C and then organise your fingers over the C, D, E, F and G notes. Practise playing these notes in many different places on the keyboard – from very low to very high and in between.

When you're comfortable playing this, make up your own melodies by rearranging the order of the notes. Have fun experimenting.

A musician friend says the reason why there are so many keys on a piano is so you have a better chance of hitting the right one occasionally!

LET'S PLAY STRAIGHT AWAY

Begin by numbering the fingers on each hand. Most music with fingering written on it refers to the thumb as 1.

RIGHT HAND

On the previous page, you placed the right hand (RH) thumb on middle C and played the next four notes with the remaining fingers. You played C, D, E, F and G with fingers 1, 2, 3, 4 and 5.

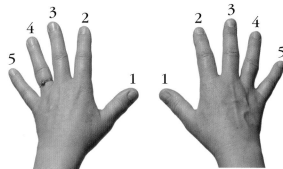

LEFT HAND

Put the fifth finger of the left hand (LH) on the C an octave below middle C and place the remaining fingers and thumb on the next four notes.

Play C, D, E, F and G with fingers 5, 4, 3, 2 and 1. Practise playing up and down to get the feel of it. Then repeat what you did with the RH and play all around the keyboard with the fifth finger always on C.

BOTH HANDS

As a general rule, the LH usually plays below middle C and the RH plays above. Of course, you can use either hand to play anywhere, but for now, this rule will help.

Exercise 1

Here's a little coordination exercise.

1 Put both thumbs on middle C.

2 Play the same fingers at the same time. The RH plays C, D, E, F and G as the LH plays C, B, A, G and F.

3 Repeat this a few times, going back and forth to become accustomed to how it feels.

This is called playing in **contrary motion**.

Exercise 2

Now you know where to put your fingers, let's play a tune we all know – *Mary Had a Little Lamb*. Try it first with both hands playing separately.

– or ——— = hold

Place the thumb of your right hand on middle C.

RH | 3 2 1 2 | 3 3 3 – | 2 2 2 – | 3 5 5 – | 3 2 1 2 | 3 3 3 3 | 2 2 3 2 | 1 ——— ‖

Place the fifth finger of your left hand on the C below middle C.

LH | 3 4 5 4 | 3 3 3 – | 4 4 4 – | 3 1 1 – | 3 4 5 4 | 3 3 3 3 | 4 4 3 4 | 5 ——— ‖

Exercise 3

If you're up for a challenge, try it with both hands playing together! In this exercise, both the fingering numbers and the note names are used.

Note name	E D C D	E E E –	D D D –	E G G –	E D C D	E E E E	D D E D	C ———
RH	3 2 1 2	3 3 3 –	2 2 2 –	3 5 5 –	3 2 1 2	3 3 3 3	2 2 3 2	1 ———
LH	3 4 5 4	3 3 3 –	4 4 4 –	3 1 1 –	3 4 5 4	3 3 3 3	4 4 3 4	5 ———

Exercise 4

Make it sound a bit nicer by accompanying the tune with some simple chords played by the LH. A chord is two or more notes played together.

1. Play C, E and G together with the LH. This chord is known as C major (or C for short).
2. Now, play B, D and G together with the LH. This chord is G (making chords and their names is addressed more thoroughly later in the book). To make this chord, you will need to move your fingers into the correct position.

Note name	E D C D	E E E –	D D D –	E G G –	E D C D	E E E E	D D E D	C ———
RH	3 2 1 2	3 3 3 –	2 2 2 –	3 5 5 –	3 2 1 2	3 3 3 3	2 2 3 2	1 ———
LH	1G ———		1G ———	1G ———	G ———		1G ———	1G ———
	3E ———		3D ———	3E ———	E ———		3D ———	3E ———
	5C ———		5B ———	5C ———	C ———		5B ———	5C ———
	C chord		**G chord**					

Exercise 5

Let's play another well-known tune: *Jingle Bells*. Apply the same method of learning this as with the previous tune – play each hand separately.

First the right hand:

Note name	E E E –	E E E –	E G C D	E ——	F F F F	F E E E	E D D E	D – G –
RH	3 3 3 –	3 3 3 –	3 5 1 2	3 ——	4 4 4 4	4 3 3 3	3 2 2 3	2 – 5 –

Note name	E E E –	E E E –	E G C D	E ——	F F F F	F E E E	G G F D	C ——
RH	3 3 3 –	3 3 3 –	3 5 1 2	3 ——	4 4 4 4	4 3 3 3	5 5 4 2	1 ——

Then the left hand:

Note name	E E E –	E E E –	E G C D	E ——	F F F F	F E E E	E D D E	D – G –
LH	3 3 3 –	3 3 3 –	3 1 5 4	3 ——	2 2 2 2	2 3 3 3	3 4 4 3	4 – 1 –

Note name	E E E –	E E E –	E G C D	E ——	F F F F	F E E E	G G F D	C ——
LH	3 3 3 –	3 3 3 –	3 1 5 4	3 ——	2 2 2 2	2 3 3 3	1 1 2 4	5 ——

Then together:

Note name	E E E –	E E E –	E G C D	E ——	F F F F	F E E E	E D D E	D – G –
RH	3 3 3 –	3 3 3 –	3 5 1 2	3 ——	4 4 4 4	4 3 3 3	3 2 2 3	2 – 5 –
LH	3 3 3 –	3 3 3 –	3 1 5 4	3 ——	2 2 2 2	2 3 3 3	3 4 4 3	4 – 1 –

Note name	E E E –	E E E –	E G C D	E ——	F F F F	F E E E	G G F D	C ——
RH	3 3 3 –	3 3 3 –	3 5 1 2	3 ——	4 4 4 4	4 3 3 3	5 5 4 2	1 ——
LH	3 3 3 –	3 3 3 –	3 1 5 4	3 ——	2 2 2 2	2 3 3 3	1 1 2 4	5 ——

Finally, with the LH accompaniment, to which we add another chord: C, F and A. This is F major. While the fingerings for two of the chords in this exercise are the same, the hand position on the keyboard is different. Here are how the C, F and G chords look when played on the keyboard.

C chord

F chord

G chord

Let's apply it to this exercise:

Note name	EEE–	EEE–	EGCD	E——	FFFF	FEEE	EDDE	D–G–
RH	3 3 3 –	3 3 3 –	3 5 1 2	3 ——	4 4 4 4	4 3 3 3	3 2 2 3	2 – 5 –
LH	1G ——	G ——	G ——		1A ——	1G ——	1G ——	
	3E ——	E ——	E ——		2F ——	3E ——	3D ——	
	5C ——	C ——	C ——		5C ——	5C ——	5B ——	

C chord (under first group)   **F chord** (under FFFF)   **G chord** (under EDDE)

Note name	EEE–	EEE–	EGCD	E——	FFFF	FEEE	GGFD	C——
RH	3 3 3 –	3 3 3 –	3 5 1 2	3 ——	4 4 4 4	4 3 3 3	5 5 4 2	1 ——
LH	1G ——	G ——	G ——		1A ——	1G ——	1G ——	1G ——
	3E ——	E ——	E ——		2F ——	3E ——	3D ——	3E ——
	5C ——	C ——	C ——		5C ——	5C ——	5B ——	5C ——

C chord (under first group)   **F chord** (under FFFF)   **G chord** (under GGFD)

Maybe you'd like to mix it up a bit by varying how you play the chords. You can hold them down, play them briefly or play them along with each note. Experiment and see what you prefer.

Exercise 6
One more to keep you busy: *Ode to Joy*.

Here's the right hand:

Note name	EEFG	GFED	CCDE	E–D–	EEFG	GFED	CCDE	D–C–
RH	3 3 4 5	5 4 3 2	1 1 2 3	3 – 2 –	3 3 4 5	5 4 3 2	1 1 2 3	2 – 1 –

And the left hand:

Note name	EEFG	GFED	CCDE	E–D–	EEFG	GFED	CCDE	D–C–
LH	3 3 2 1	1 2 3 4	5 5 4 3	3 – 4 –	3 3 2 1	1 2 3 4	5 5 4 3	4 – 5 –

Now let's play it with both hands:

Note name	EEFG	GFED	CCDE	E-D-	EEFG	GFED	CCDE	D-C-
RH	3345	5432	1123	3-2-	3345	5432	1123	2-1-
LH	3321	1234	5543	3-4-	3321	1234	5543	4-5-

And finally with chords played with the left hand. Accompanying chords are C major and G major only.

Note name	EEFG	GFED	CCDE	E- D-	EEFG	GFED	CCDE	D- C-
RH	3345	5432	1123	3- 2-	3345	5432	1123	2- 1-
LH	1G——	1G——	1G——	1G–1G–	1G——	1G——	1G——	1G–1G–
	3E——	3D——	3E——	3E–3D–	3E——	3D——	3E——	3D–3E–
	5C——	5B——	5C——	5C–5B–	5C——	5B——	5C——	5B–5C–

Try to not be hard on yourself if you don't get it first time. If you've never played before, it will seem quite foreign to your hands. If you were taking weekly lessons from a teacher, you'd be given these exercises in your first lesson and left to practise for a week before moving on, so give it time. You'll be surprised how quickly you pick it up.

Exercise 7

If you want to play chords to accompany a singer or yourself singing a song, here's a great way to start. These exercises use the three chords you've learned so far (C, F and G).

1 Start with the LH thumb on C and play the C chord with the RH. Notice the C chord fingering changes depending on which chord follows it. From C to F is 1, 2 and 4 (photo 1), which lets the fingers flow to the F chord. However, before playing a G chord, the C chord fingering is 1, 3 and 5 (photo 2). This stops you jumping around the keys too much.

2 With the LH fifth finger on F, play the F chord with the RH (photo 3).

3 With the LH fourth finger on G, play the G chord with the RH (photo 4).

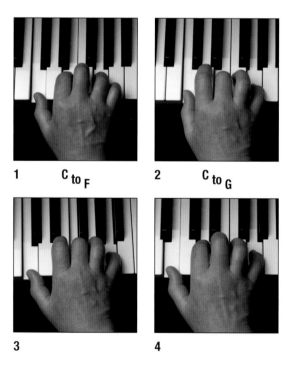

1   C to F   2   C to G

3   4

C chord with different fingering

RH	4G – G G	5A – A A	5G – G G	5G – G G	4G – G G	5A – A A	5G G 5G G	5G ——
	2E – E E	3F – F F	3E – E E	2D – D D	2E – E E	3F – F F	3E E 2D D	3E ——
	1C – C C	1C – C C	1C – C C	1B – B B	1C – C C	1C – C C	1C C 1B B	1C ——

LH	C – CC	F – FF	C – CC	G – GG	C – CC	F – FF	CC GG	C ——

This exercise has the hands playing at different times.

X = don't play

RH	X G X G	X A X A	X G X G	X G X G	X G X G	X A X A	X G X G	G ——
	X E X E	X F X F	X E X E	X D X D	X E X E	X F X F	X E X D	E ——
	X C X C	X C X C	X C X C	X B X B	X C X C	X C X C	X C X B	C ——

LH	C – C –	F – F –	C – C –	G – G –	C – C –	F – F –	C – G –	C ——

It's amazing how many songs are written on just these three chords.

LEARNING SCALES AND LISTENING

C MAJOR SCALE

The simplest scale on the piano is C major. It is made up of all the white keys, starting on C and ending on the next C. It's really, really, really (get my point!) important to use the correct fingering for this, because if you don't, you'll never be able to play well, even for the simplest of melodies.

The fingering is 1, 2, 3, 1, 2, 3, 4, 5 for RH ascending and 5, 4, 3, 2, 1, 3, 2, 1 for LH ascending.

Practise swinging the thumb under the third finger. Try playing up and down the D, E, F and G section of the scale to get used to it.

POSITION AND NOTE NAMES IN THE SCALE

Get used to naming the notes as you play them and to their position in the scale. In the C major scale, C=1, D=2, E=3, F=4, G=5, A=6 and B=7.

It's important that you are familiar with the note names and numbers, as they are referred to both ways.

You can also learn the scale using a method called **Solfège**, which is a system that names the notes of the ascending scale as Doh (C), Re (D), Mi (E), Fa (F), So (G), La (A), Ti (B) and Doh (C).

CHORDS AND SCALE DEGREES

Look at the scale of C on the keyboard. You should now be able to just look at the keys and 'see' the scale.

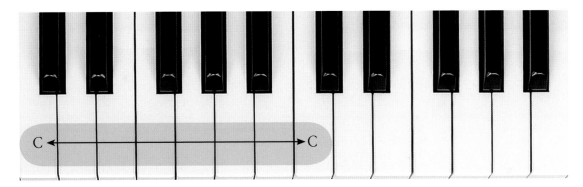

Play the scale degrees of 1, 3 and 5 (every second note) with the fingers 1, 3 and 5 of the RH. They sound pleasant. Now play them together – we did this in the last lesson with the LH and know it is called the chord of C major.

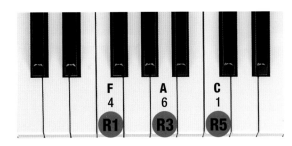

Now find F, or the fourth degree, and play every second note – F, A and C (use fingers 1, 3 and 5). We also did this in the last lesson and it is called F major.

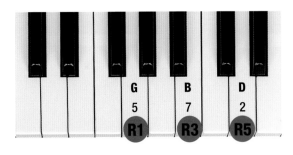

Now do the same with the fifth degree – G, B, D. This chord is called G major.

You can build chords anywhere on the piano doing this. Try it for each note on the C major scale, using the same hand position. (For your interest, the chords you will play are C major, D minor, E minor, F major, G major, A minor and B diminished.)

Piano is great for this, as you can see everything clearly on the keyboard, unlike stringed instruments, for example, where you can play the same note two or more ways.

Play these chords with the RH. To give it a fuller sound, play the **bass note** of the chord with the LH. The bass note of a chord gives the chord its name. For example:
• C major has C as its bass note.
• D minor has D as its bass note.
The note is always played lower on the keyboard than the rest of the chord. Bass always refers to low notes.

Here is the C major chord and its bass note:

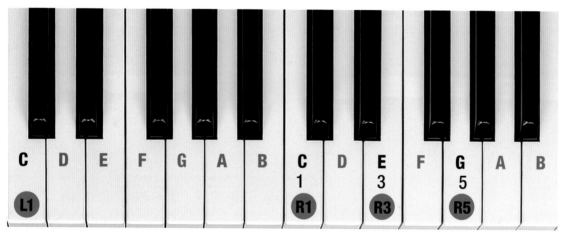

Get used to the feel and the sound of the chords. Play them in different orders all over the piano, and listen to how the sound changes depending on where you play them. This is how you begin to develop your ear. Eventually you'll be able to recognise which scale degree and what chord you are hearing.

Go back to pages 15–19 and try to learn *Mary Had a Little Lamb, Jingle Bells* and *Ode to Joy* by heart. When you have done this, think about the scale degrees you're playing and what the chord is.

OTHER MAJOR SCALES

All major scales sound similar, no matter where you start from on the piano. You can build all the major scales (there's only 12 of them) from each other – it's really easy.

Exercise 8

1. Play C major scale all the way up to the D above the C at the top of the octave. Don't worry about the right fingering for now.
2. Put your thumb onto the G and start to play using the same fingering as for the scale of C.
3. The only thing that changes is that you have to play the black note the fourth finger is about to play at **scale degree 7** (the left of the group of three black notes). This note is called F sharp. The scale is called G major.

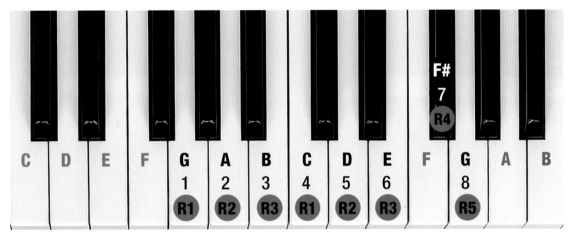

If you'd like a challenge, build scales starting on D, A and E using the same method. These scales have been selected because you keep adding a new black note at scale degree number 7, as well as playing the sharps from the previous scale.
• G major has one sharp: F#.
• D major has two sharps: F# and C#.
• A major has three sharps: F#, C# and G#.
• E major has four sharps: F#, C#, G# and D#.
Notice how each time a sharp is added, it is five letter names away from the previous one.

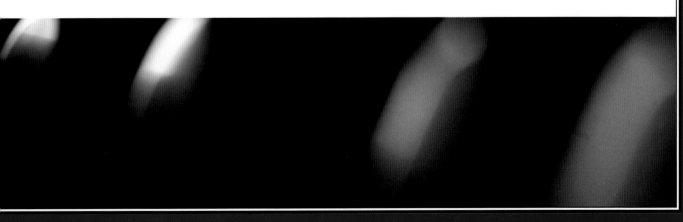

Exercise 9

The **D major** scale has **two sharps**.

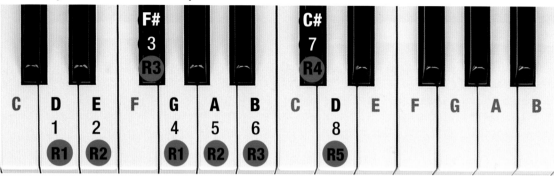

Exercise 10

The **A major** scale has **three sharps**.

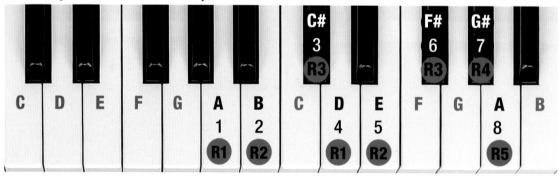

Exercise 11

The **E major** scale has **four sharps**.

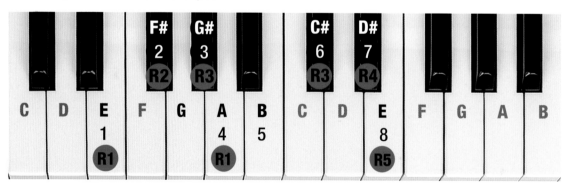

Reading Music Made Easy I

Written music deals with three concepts:
- **pitch** (which notes to play)
- **time** (when to play the notes) and
- **space** (when not to play).

We need to be able to easily represent these three things graphically.

A Possible Way of Representing Music

Let's go back to *Ode to Joy*. It could be written like this:

	1	2	3	4	1	2	3	4
4	E	E	F	G	G	F	E	D

	1	2	3	4	1	2	3	4
	C	C	D	E	E	—	D	—

————— 1 bar ————— ————— 1 bar —————

The notes are grouped in fours because this is how the natural accents occur in this piece of music. Each note falls on a **beat**. Each of the divisions of 4 is called a **bar** (or a measure). The 4 at the start tells the reader that there are **4 beats** in each **bar**.

This only shows the melody without the chords. To show the chords as we played them earlier could look like this:

RH	E	E	F	G	G	F	E	D
LH	G				G			
	E				D			
	C				B			

RH	C	C	D	E	E	—	D	—
LH	G				G		G	
	E				E		D	
	C				C		B	

While this system looks adequate, it is actually incomplete because, although it tells us the notes, it doesn't tell us which octave they are played in. Thankfully, a great system has evolved over centuries of music making.

THE ELEMENTS OF WRITING MUSIC

WRITING THE PITCH

The pitches are written on five lines called the **staff** or **stave**.

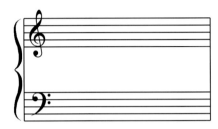

Piano music is typically written with two staves – one showing the **treble** (high pitches) and one showing the **bass** (low pitches). This is done using a **treble clef** and a **bass clef**.

WRITING THE TIME

As with the first possible example, the stave is divided up into bars with a number at the start.

This is the **time signature**.
- The top number indicates how many beats there are in a bar.
- The bottom number indicates what type of beat it is.

Piano music...

4/4 is such a frequently used time signature that some music has a C as the time signature, meaning **common time** or 4/4.

PUTTING PITCH AND TIME TOGETHER

Instead of using letter names, notes are used to show which keys to play on the piano.

Middle
C D E F G A B C

Using this information, we can write the right hand of *Ode to Joy* like this:

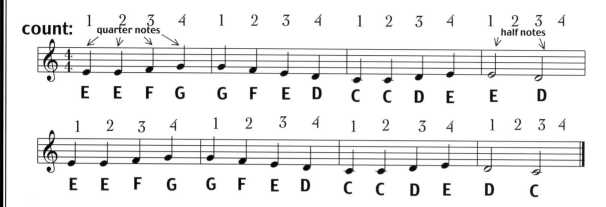

Notice that whenever you count '1', you're beginning a new bar. The type of notes used here are called **quarter notes** and **half notes**. In this piece of music, the quarter notes are worth one beat each and the half notes are worth two beats each.

• The top 4 indicates that there are 4 beats in the bar.
• The bottom 4 indicates that the type of beat is a quarter note.

There are 4 quarter notes in each bar. (Notice the bar with the two half notes still adds up to 4 beats.)

REPRESENTING WHAT THE LEFT HAND PLAYS

Instead of using letter names, like in the first possible example, notes are used to show which keys to play on the piano.

We need to show what the left hand plays. This could be done by just adding notes under the stave, but they would be so far below the stave that they would be too hard to read.

We have to add another stave with a bass clef to indicate that this part of the music is played lower down on the keyboard. To fully write what you've previously played with *Ode to Joy*, you end up with:

As with all good things, plenty of practice makes reading music easier. Don't be discouraged if this seems like a lot to learn. Take your time – there's no rush. Count to yourself or out loud before playing so you know how fast you're going to play and how many beats there are in each bar.

THE LINES AND SPACES ON A STAVE

It is important to accustom yourself to the names of the lines and spaces in the stave. The names are different on the treble and bass staves.

There is an easy way to remember this. On the treble stave, the lines read **E**, **G**, **B**, **D** and **F**. A simple rhyme is often used to remember this: **E**very **G**ood **B**oy **D**eserves **F**ruit.

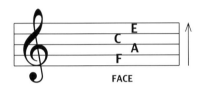

Running upwards, the spaces spell **FACE**.

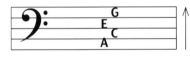

There is a similar way to remember the lines of the bass clef. **G**, **B**, **D**, **F** and **A** become **G**ood **B**oys **D**eserve **F**ruit **A**lways.

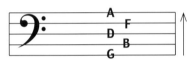

The spaces of the bass clef are **A**, **C**, **E** and **G**, which become **A**ll **C**ows **E**at **G**rass.

Refer back to page 15 to see how *Mary Had a Little Lamb* was previously written out. This is how it appears in music notation.

LEGER LINES

We've looked at the notes that are 'in' the stave, but we also have to write notes on the stave that fall above or below the five lines and four spaces. To do this, we use **leger lines**. They look like this:

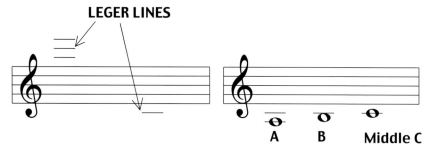

To write middle C in the treble clef and the A and B that precede it, the notes are placed on leger lines below the stave.

WRITING THE SPACE

We've seen how to write time and pitch, but how do we write space? Just as we use a note to show pitch and what beat we play that pitch on, we also need to show where to play nothing. To do this, we use a symbol called a **rest**. A rest indicates where not to play.

• A quarter note rest indicates that you don't play for the same length of time as a quarter note.
• A half note rest indicates that you don't play for the same length of time as a half note.

PUTTING PITCH, TIME AND SPACE TOGETHER

Try playing this simple melody noticing the rests and using the correct fingering:

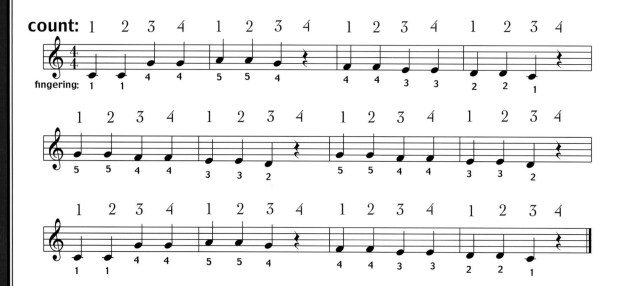

Have a look at this piece in **3/4 time**. Remember:
• the top number (3) shows how many beats in the bar
• the bottom number (4) shows the type of beats.
In this piece of music, there are 3 quarter note beats in each bar. Use the correct fingering and notice the use of two quarter note rests and one half note rest. The new note introduced here is a dotted half note. It is held for 3 beats.

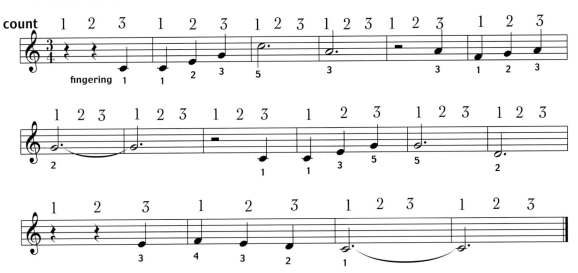

Notice that in some bars, two quarter note rests are used to show two beats of silence and elsewhere a half note rest is used to show the same amount of silence. This is so you can see both kinds of rest being used.

Some popular musical manuscripts also show chord names above the melody instead of using the bass clef.

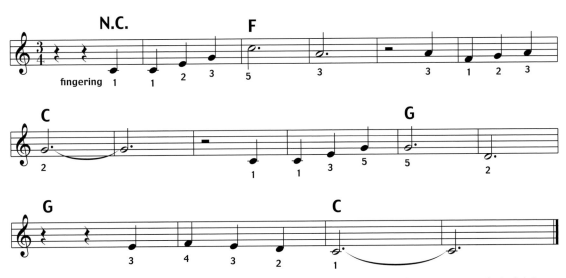

Usually this is done when a guitarist or other musician plays along, but it's just as helpful for the pianist who doesn't read the bass clef quite as well as the treble clef. When you buy the sheet music of a popular song, it is often represented this way.

READING MUSIC MADE EASY II

On pages 27–31 we looked at quarter and half notes, the time signatures of 3/4 and 4/4, the stave (or staff), treble and bass clefs and rests.

WRITING NOTES

The writing of music has 'grammar' in much the same way that a language has. In fact, music is a written language and is the only truly universal form of communication.

So far you've read and played all the white notes on the piano and can write a scale of C major like this:

Written notes are made up of the head and the stem. Notice that the stem sits on a different side of the note, depending on whether it is pointing up or down. Also notice that before B the stems point up, and after they point down. This is so the stems stay within the stave and it is neater and easier to read.

SHARPS AND FLATS

Sharps and **flats** are used to show the black notes. To cancel a sharp or flat, use a **natural sign**.

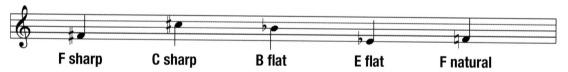

Let's look at the black notes on the keyboard and name them. The first thing to remember is that when you go **up** to a black note, it is named after the white note to its left plus the **sharp** sign.

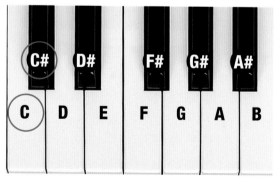

For example, find a C on the keyboard. The black note to the right of it (upwards) is C# (C sharp). F# is the black note to the right of F and G# is the black note to the right of G. It's the same for the other notes.

For **flats**, go **down** from a white note to a black. When you go down to a black note, it is named after the white note to its right plus the flat sign.

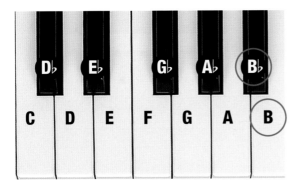

Find a B on the keyboard. The B♭ must be the black note just to its left. Here A♭ is the black note to the left of A and G♭ is the black note to the left of G. The same applies for the other notes.

You may have realised by now that the black notes can have two names – for example, C♯ is the same as D♭. Without going into too much detail, the name you use depends on which scale is used. However, the most important thing is that you can find them on a keyboard.

MORE NOTE LENGTHS

There are another couple of note lengths that you need to know:

       whole note   **dotted half note**

- the **whole note**, which is worth four beats
- the **dotted half note**, which is worth three beats.

So now we have four different note lengths:
- whole notes (four beats)
- half notes (two beats)
- dotted half notes (three beats)
- quarter notes (one beat).

Here is a way of showing varying note lengths in a bar of 4/4 time.

Here's one more note length: the **eighth note**. It is half the length of the quarter note and is written like this:

To make it easier to read them, eighth notes are grouped together if there are two or more in a row. They are connected with a beam.

Here's another example of combined note lengths. Notice how the total of beats in each bar adds up to 4 – the top number in the time signature.

MORE RESTS

Remember, just as we need to show note lengths, we also need to show rest lengths, or how long we don't play. Here are all the rests in order of length (or value):

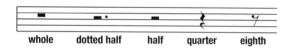

whole   dotted half   half   quarter   eighth

- whole rest (four beats)
- half rest (two beats)
- dotted half rest (three beats)
- quarter rest (one beat)
- eighth rest (half a beat).

THE TIE

A tie is used to join the lengths of two or more notes of the same pitch together to make one long note. The tied notes can be the same or different lengths. The length of the long note equals the value of each note added together.

See this example of *On Top of Old Smokey*. It shows notes of different lengths joined (tied) together.

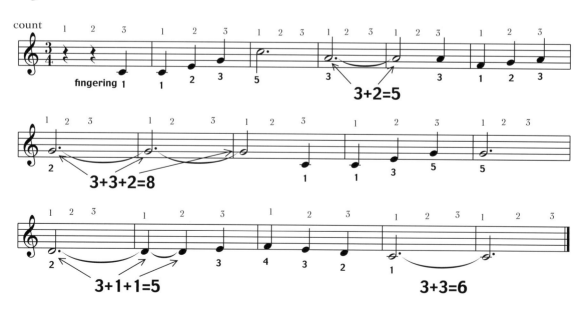

PUTTING IT ALL TOGETHER

The following example shows different combinations of rhythms using rests, notes and ties. Just one pitch is used to help you focus on only reading rhythms, not pitch. Make sure you count the beats as you play through this exercise.

Example in 4/4 time

Example in 3/4 time

EXERCISES FOR FINGER INDEPENDENCE

If you've never played piano, it is important to teach your fingers to operate independently and in ways they haven't before. The following exercises are designed to build the dexterity of your fingers. Although these exercises are written for two hands, it is important to master each hand separately before playing with both hands. Don't be in a hurry to play with both hands together or you may pick up some bad habits. Play slowly and accurately until you have mastered the exercises and make sure you are lifting the fingers.

Learn to play the exercises by heart, as it's fun to sit at the piano and play without written music. Most importantly, you can watch your fingers and check your technique.

Exercise 12

The fourth and fifth fingers especially need to be worked as they share the same tendon. The fourth finger is the weakest, so here is an exercise to strengthen it.

Exercise 13

This five-finger exercise starts like a scale.

Exercise 14

This seemingly simple exercise will build your finger independence. Always play this one slowly – it's not a speed exercise. Hold your thumbs down while playing the other notes.

Exercise 15

This exercise focuses on strengthening the third, fourth and fifth fingers and builds their independence. The repeating pattern works its way up the scale one way and down the scale a second way. Instead of reading every note, learn the pattern and see where it starts, changes and finishes.

Exercise 16

Only emphasise finger lifting when playing an exercise. Finger lifting helps with accuracy on the keys, but less effort should be used when playing anything else on the piano.

A group of notes played together at the same time can form a **chord**. For example, playing C, E and G together sounds great. If you play these same notes one after the other (C, E and then G), you are playing an **arpeggio**, or a 'broken chord'.

This last exercise spreads the fingers, helping build accuracy for playing chords and arpeggios.

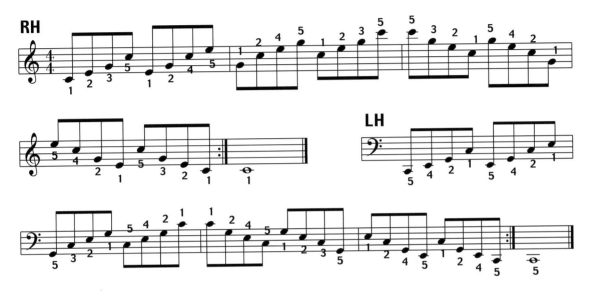

Once you've mastered more piano techniques, use these exercises as a basis to create your own. For example, turn majors into minors or play in another key (this is covered later in the lesson).

PLAY SOME POPULAR CLASSICS

It is very beneficial to play classical music on the piano because, unlike most popular music, classical pieces help you maintain good technique and not fall into bad habits. Classical music requires more technically, plus it keeps playing interesting because of the huge number of different styles that can be found.

Play a scale of G major, noticing the F# at the seventh degree.

fingering 1   2   3   1   2   3   4   5

MINUET, BACH

Now let's play a popular classic by Bach in G major. This piece requires a shift in hand position. It is always good to work out the fingering before you start to play as the music will flow better. If you buy a book of simple piano pieces, the author will usually indicate good fingering choices.

This piece is in 3/4 time, which means three quarter notes in every bar. 3/4 is often known as waltz time.

To keep it simple and to avoid having to write the sharp sign before every F note, it is indicated at the beginning of the stave that every F is actually an F#. This is called the **key signature**.

The key signature shows that all Fs are actually F sharps

Arr. R. Payne

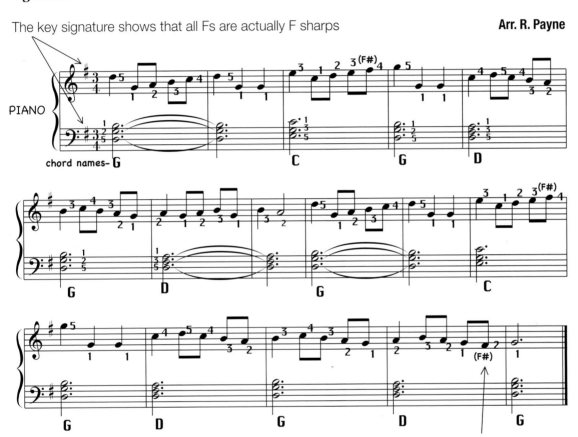

Notice how the first phrase falls under the five fingers. Then you move to the next position where the five fingers cover the notes you need. You should be able to play an octave easily with the thumb and the fifth finger.

Now is a good time to introduce a new chord: D major. You have played the chords of C major, F major and G major, and they were referred to as the chords built on the 1st, 4th and 5th scale degrees.

We are now doing the same thing, but in the scale of G major instead of C major. The chords on the 1st, 4th and 5th degrees are G major, C major and D major respectively.

The second finger crosses over the thumb to play F# in the second last bar.

Here is another way to play this piece involving the left hand more.

Arr. R. Payne

This style of arpeggiated bass is called **Alberti Bass**. It creates more movement than just playing a straight chord in each bar.

Another two popular piano solo pieces are the *Blue Danube Waltz* by Strauss and *Für Elise* by Beethoven.

BLUE DANUBE WALTZ, STRAUSS

Arr. R. Payne

Für Elise, Beethoven

Arr. R. Payne

PIANO

pedal on   pedal off

See how you have to move your hand to another position in order to play smoothly from one note to the next. These two pieces are great for learning how to move your hands around the keyboard. Once you know how to play the notes, try this with the sustain (right) pedal where marked.

PRACTICE TECHNIQUE

Now that you've moved to a slightly more difficult and longer piece, it's a good time to look at practice techniques. There are very few pianists who have success with their piano playing by just running through a piece of music a few times. Instead, there will have been hours and hours of practice time (and it is usually well-organised practice time).

One invaluable tool to help with practice technique is a metronome. Metronomes can be either mechanical or electronic and provide a steady pulse at varying speeds to practise to.

Although practice techniques, such as the following, may feel like they make it take longer to learn a piece of music, I know from experience that they actually save time and encourage accuracy in your playing.

For example, if you wanted to learn a piece for a concert, you would need to organise your practice so you could gradually improve on the different parts of the music while keeping track of your progress. Here is how I apply this to a practice session:

1. Break a piece into four-bar sections. Play the first four bars slowly using a metronome. Find a speed at which you can play it without faltering. Repeat those four bars a few times.
2. If there's a particular place where you always stumble, turn off the metronome and work at the troublesome part slowly.
3. When you think you have mastered it, play it again with the metronome.
4. Now put these four bars aside and do the same with the next four. Only work on eight or twelve bars in one practice session and mark down your metronome setting when you finish.
5. Start the next practice session at that same metronome setting. If you play without mistakes, raise the speed by one degree. This speed change should be barely noticeable. Don't raise it by more than one degree per practice session.
6. As you continue to raise the speed, you'll find your limit. Play at this tempo for a while. By continuing to be disciplined and not raising the speed until everything is perfect, you'll have learnt a piece both accurately and permanently.

If you don't have a metronome, you can still practise like this. Keep your counting steady and only increase the tempo once you feel you've mastered it.

Many people aim for speed instead of accuracy. Remember, a listener will notice how terrible a fast sloppy performance is, but rarely will they notice anything bad about a slower, more accurate one. There is an old saying that 'practice makes perfect', but a better one is 'practice makes permanent'.

ACCOMPANIMENT USING BASS AND CHORDS

The piano is often used to accompany a singer or a solo instrument. A good way to study piano as an accompaniment to popular songs or for your own compositions is to listen to some of your favourite artists. For example, an artist such as Elton John plays great piano accompaniments to popular rock songs or ballads. Listen closely to some tunes featuring piano and focus on what the pianist is doing.

POPULAR MUSIC

The great thing about piano is that you have almost the equivalent of a whole band at your fingertips. In popular music there is usually:
• a drum part, often consisting of at least a bass drum and a snare drum
• a bass part, played on the bass guitar or a double bass
• some type of chord playing, performed on a guitar and/or a piano or keyboard.

The easiest way to play a piano accompaniment for popular music is to use:
• the left hand for the bass part and the bass drum rhythm
• the right hand for the chords, the snare drum and the guitar rhythms, emphasising the beat.

The most common time signatures used in popular music are 4/4, 3/4 and 6/8. 6/8 time consists of 6 eighth note beats per bar and it has a flowing, swaying lilt to it, which can be felt in the old song *Daisy, Daisy, Give Me Your Answer True*.
Here is an example of a simple pop tune with the chords played in root position.

The LH plays the bass part with a similar rhythm to a bass drum and the RH plays the same rhythm as a snare drum.

CHORD INVERSIONS

This brings us to **voicing**. If I played the chords in this song in **root position** (called root position because they're built up from the root of the scale they belong to, such as building chords in C major using 1, 3 and 5), I'd be moving my hands all around the piano. It would eventually sound odd and distracting to the listener.

You can make it sound better by using **inversions** of chords. A chord inversion is the same notes of a chord rearranged in a different order. Using inversions means the hands move easily from one chord to another because they are in the one position.

(Chord inversions happen automatically when a guitarist plays the common chord shapes – you rarely hear a guitarist playing all chords in root position.)

You should also notice when playing chords that the right hand usually plays more notes than the left hand. Good chord voicings have more space between the lower notes, preventing the music from sounding muddy. We'll be using the left hand to mainly play bass parts.

So now I would play this song like this:

To make the tune flow more, I should put in some other rhythms that are less heavy than the snare drum beat: a bit more like what the guitar would play.

Let's now look at accompanying a ballad. I'll play it on the piano as I did the last song using root chords on every snare drum beat.

This sounds a bit stodgy and lumpy without flow. A nicer way to do it would be to think like the guitarist again, and arpeggiate the chords as well as play them in inversions so they flow together nicely.

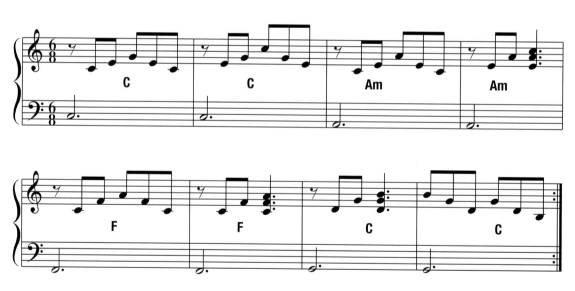

Practise playing along to a metronome – it will help you to 'lock in' to the feel.

Remember that you can play a pop accompaniment by using chords, or arpeggiating, or a combination of both.

You can also make the piano sound bigger by using octaves in the bass like this.

C CHORD

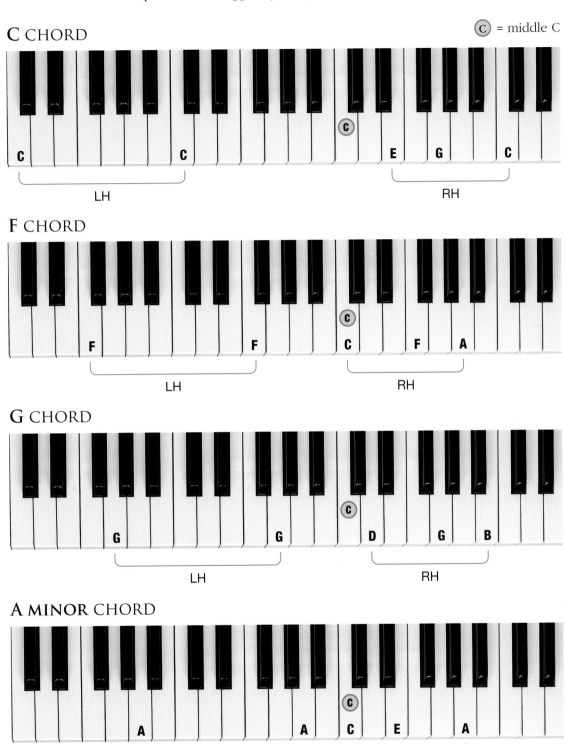

ⓒ = middle C

F CHORD

G CHORD

A MINOR CHORD

BOOGIE PIANO

B oogie (or boogie-woogie) piano is a blues style that is upbeat and happy, in contrast with the blues, which is usually slower and more melancholy. It is most easily recognised by its repeating bass line played in eighth notes (or quavers). Here's another easy tune to play with the right hand while the left hand learns a boogie piano style.

Exercise 17

Play *Oh When the Saints* with the right hand until you are familiar with it so you can concentrate on the left hand. This is an easy five-finger melody, so once you know it, you won't even have to watch your right hand.

Boogie piano styles vary enormously. Here are a few simple ideas to get you started. These examples use the three most common major chords, which are C, F and G, or, if using their scale degrees, the 1, 4 and 5 chords of C major.

Exercise 18

1. With the left hand, place the fifth finger on C and the first finger on G and play four beats per bar for three bars. This is the C chord.

2. Play D with the fourth finger and G with the first finger. Play four beats per bar for one bar. This is the G chord.

3. Again, place the fifth finger on C and the first finger on G and play the C chord for four beats per bar for two bars.

4. Play C with the fifth finger and F with the second for the F chord. Play four beats per bar for one bar.

5. Play the C chord for 2 beats and then play the G chord for two beats.

6. Finish with the C chord, playing two beats and then one longer note held for two beats.

Exercise 19
Once you feel comfortable playing the first left-hand exercise, try playing *Oh When the Saints* over this new left-hand pattern.

Exercise 20
This exercise uses eighth notes, which means the left hand is doing twice as much.

Exercise 21

As an accompaniment, you can use both hands like this for a nice full sound.

Try it in different positions.

Try playing this in other keys like G major and F major to learn more chords and develop listening skills. Do everything that we've just done in C and work your way through it step by step.

Another interesting boogie style is the moving bass part. This is a simple starter. Use the same fingering for each chord. This exercise introduces three new notes in the LH: D#, A# and G#. Notice the **repeat signs**. The ||: :|| symbols indicate that you should play each bar surrounded by repeat signs twice.

Play the major chords over the top of this to get both hands used to playing it.

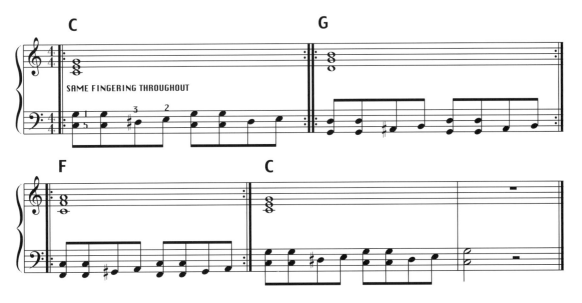

Try playing this one with a bounce.

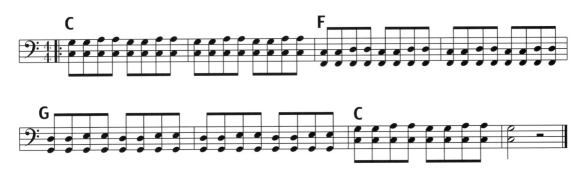

Now try playing with the chords over it in the right hand.

In this exercise, play the right hand chords in different rhythms.

Finally, here are two great boogie bass lines that you can't do without!

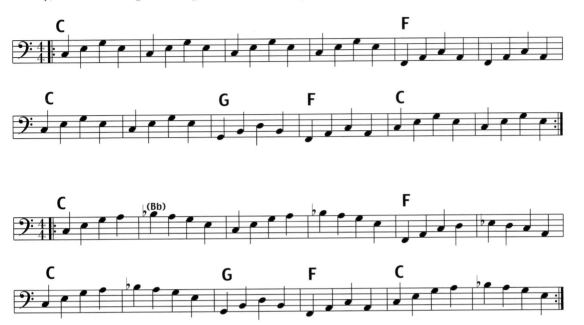

USING THE PEDALS

soft pedal   **sostenuto pedal**   **sustain pedal**
(see page 7)

THE SOFT PEDAL

There is no such thing as a 'loud' pedal on a piano. There is, however, a **soft pedal**, which is the left pedal. It is also called the **una corda** pedal and it is pressed with the left foot.

Using the soft pedal is easy: you press it when playing a very soft passage of music. As well as making the notes played softer, the tone of the notes becomes very delicate.

THE SUSTAIN PEDAL

The **sustain pedal** is the pedal to the right, and it is played with the right foot.

Using the sustain pedal requires co-ordination. To use the sustain pedal when playing chords:

1. Press the sustain pedal with your foot as you play a chord.
2. Hold the pedal down for the length of time you play the one chord.
3. As you are changing chords, lift the pedal momentarily.
4. Press down the sustain pedal again when you move on to the next chord.

If you don't lift the pedal for a change of chord, you get a very mushy and indistinct type of sound, which isn't very pleasant.

Experiment with this – you will be able to hear what sounds good and what does not.

CHORD PROGRESSIONS

H ere are some chords to learn and to have fun playing around with rhythmically. On guitar, notes (such as middle C, for example) can be played in more than one position. Therefore a diagram (called a chord shape) is often necessary in guitar music to indicate the correct hand position to use when playing the chord. But on the piano a particular note occurs only once, so we can use notes on a stave to show the exact position of chords.

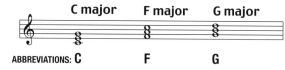

Chords are often indicated in shorthand in written music. For example, G major is written as G and F major is written as F. A letter on its own indicates a major chord in that key.

MINOR CHORDS

So far we have only looked at major chords. A **minor** chord is made by lowering the **third note** of the chord by one **semitone**. Remember, a semitone is the smallest division on the piano. It is the distance from one key to the very next one, regardless whether it is black or white.

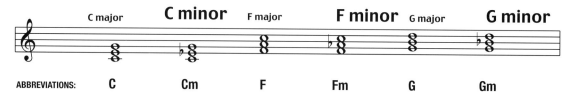

C MINOR

The chord of C major is written as C. You would play the notes C, E and G. The notes in this order are called **root position**. E is the third note of the chord, no matter what order they are played in.

To make C minor, lower E (the third note) by one semitone. The next note below E is E♭. A C minor chord would therefore be played as C, E♭ and G and is abbreviated as Cm. Use the same fingering for major or minor chords.

Chords derive their names from the **bass** note (the **tonic** or **root** note – C in this example). The names of chords always relate back to the major scale even if they're minor.

G MINOR

Play a G major chord: G, B and D.

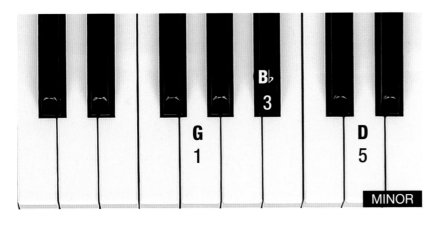

Lower the third note, B, by one semitone to B♭ and you have G minor. It is abbreviated as Gm.

F MINOR

The same formula applies to F (and all chords). Play an F major chord: F, A and C.

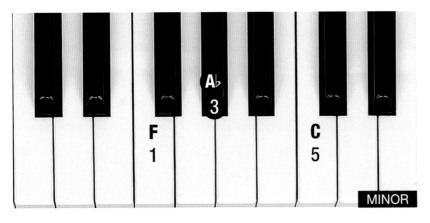

Lower the third note, A, by a semitone to A♭ and you have F minor, which is abbreviated as Fm.

USEFUL CHORD PROGRESSIONS

Here are some useful chord progressions. A chord progression is playing one or a series of chords in a sequence. Note the repeat symbols: practise playing and repeating the exercises until you feel comfortable moving from one chord to another.

‖: $\frac{4}{4}$ Dm G | Dm G | C Am | C Am :‖

‖: $\frac{4}{4}$ D F#m | G A | D F#m | Bm A :‖

The following chord progressions are often used in pop and rock music.

‖: $\frac{4}{4}$ D A | E F#m :‖

‖: $\frac{4}{4}$ F#m D | A E :‖

‖: $\frac{4}{4}$ A C | D E | A | F E :‖

‖: $\frac{4}{4}$ Am G | F E | Am C | D E :‖

‖: $\frac{6}{8}$ C | Am | F | G :‖

FOUR-NOTE CHORDS

So far we've looked at three-note chords. Remember how we made them by playing every second note in the scale.

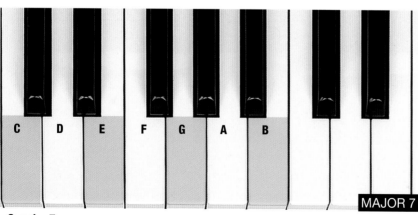

Following the same pattern of playing every second note, add a fourth note to create a four-note chord. In this case, this is a C major 7. (Note that a major 7 chord is different to a 7 chord.)

C major 7

Just as we did with the three-note chords, you can play like this all the way up the scale with four-note chords. Here are the other four-note chords in the scale of C major.

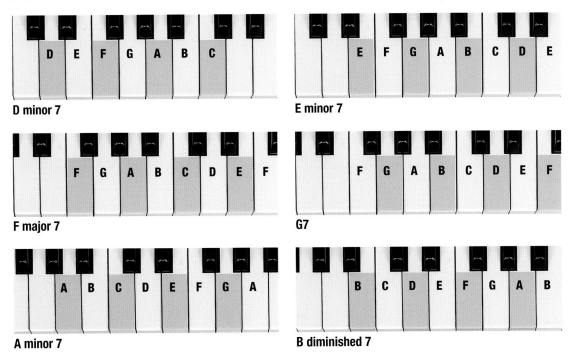

D minor 7

E minor 7

F major 7

G7

A minor 7

B diminished 7

These chords have a lovely rich sound and work beautifully when voiced nicely. Play around with them and find the ones you think are most pleasant. These sets of seven chords belong to a specific scale known as **diatonic chords**.

ALTERNATE BASS CHORDS

As well as playing the chords, you can play different bass notes against chords.

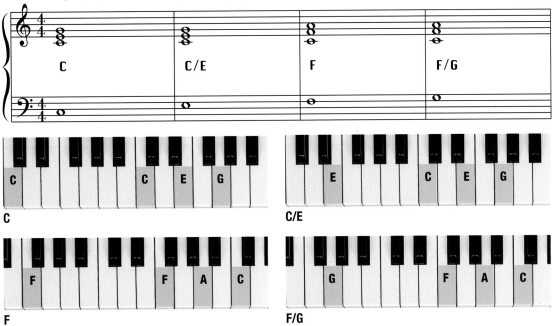

C   C/E   F   F/G

C

C/E

F

F/G

To play a progression of chords with the same bass note is a technique borrowed from classical music called a **pedal**. This is different from using the piano pedals and comes from the time when organ playing was popular. The organist held down a bass pedal while changing harmonies on the keyboard.

If you were to 'pedal a C' over all these chord changes, it would mean this:

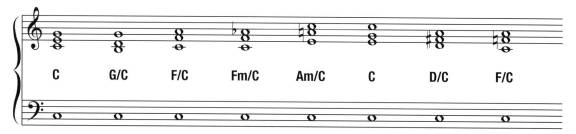

A beautiful example of the pedal technique is at the end of Bach's *Prelude in C Major*.

Here are some more popular chord progressions.

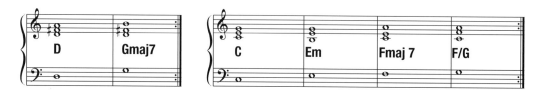

To help develop your ear, choose a chord progression and transpose it into other keys. For example, Am–Am/G–Fmaj7–E would move down a tone to Gm–Gm/F–E♭maj7–D.

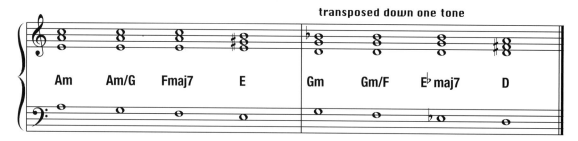

Take notice of the relationship between the chords – it stays the same no matter where you move it.

To find a chord you're not sure of, see the list of chords that follows. Most notes and chords have two names; I have listed the most commonly used names.

CHORD FINDER

C CHORD

Major

Minor

Major 7

Minor 7

7
(or dom7)

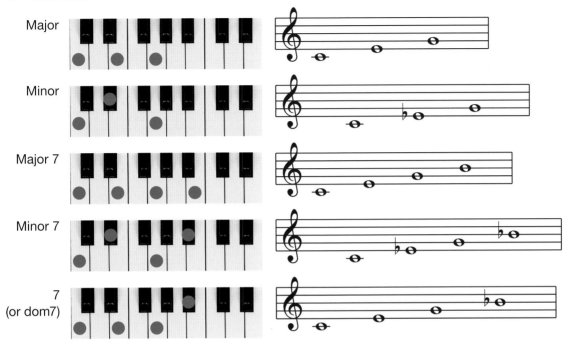

Db/C# CHORDS

Major

Minor

Major 7

Minor 7

7
(or dom7)

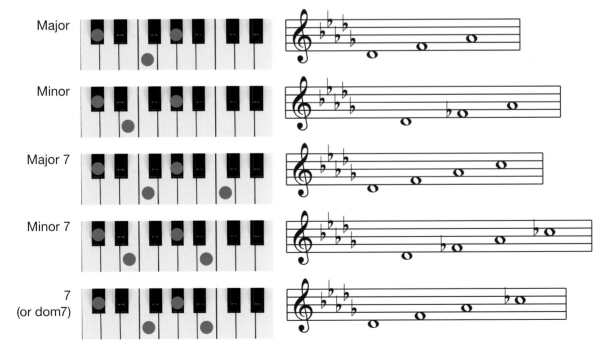

Chord Finder

D Chords

Major

Minor

Major 7

Minor 7

7
(or dom7)

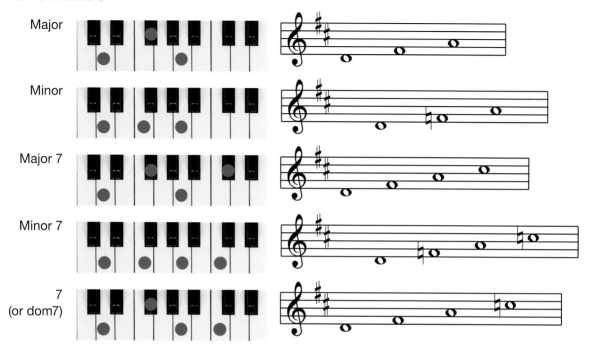

E♭/D# Chords

Major

Minor

Major 7

Minor 7

7
(or dom7)

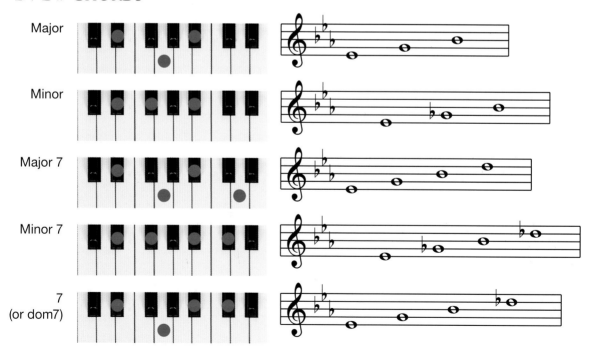

E CHORDS

Major

Minor

Major 7

Minor 7

7
(or dom7)

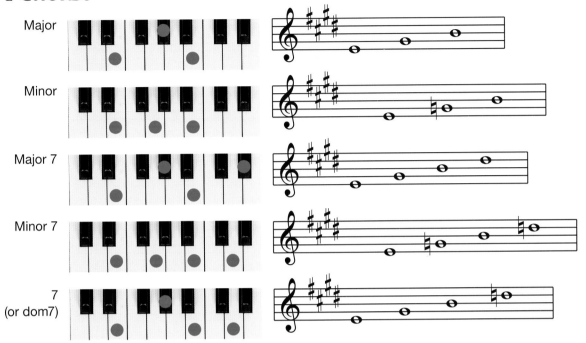

F CHORDS

Major

Minor

Major 7

Minor 7

7
(or dom7)

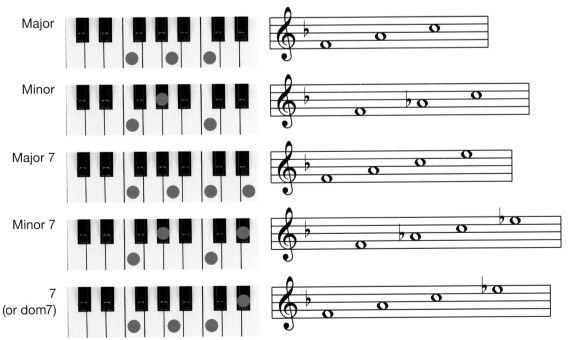

CHORD FINDER

G♭/F# CHORDS

Major

Minor

Major 7

Minor 7

7
(or dom7)

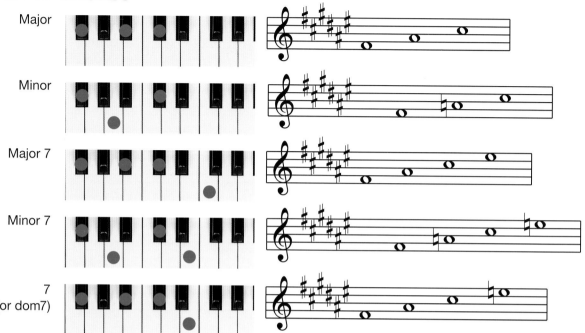

G CHORDS

Major

Minor

Major 7

Minor 7

7
(or dom7)

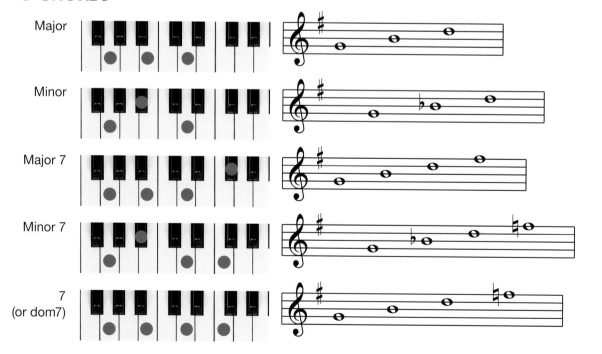

A♭/G# Chords

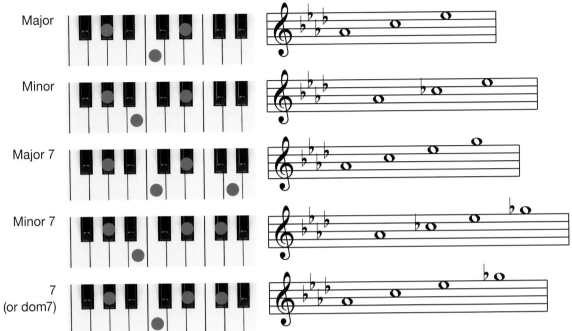

Major

Minor

Major 7

Minor 7

7
(or dom7)

A Chords

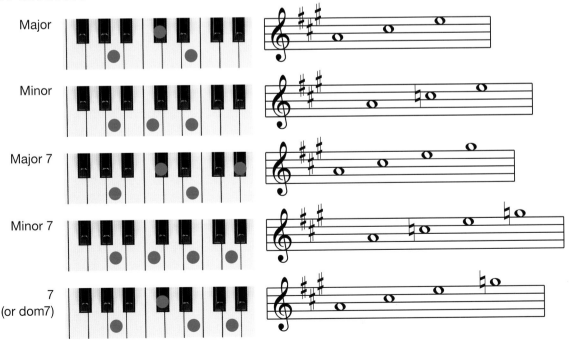

Major

Minor

Major 7

Minor 7

7
(or dom7)

Chord Finder

B♭/A# Chords

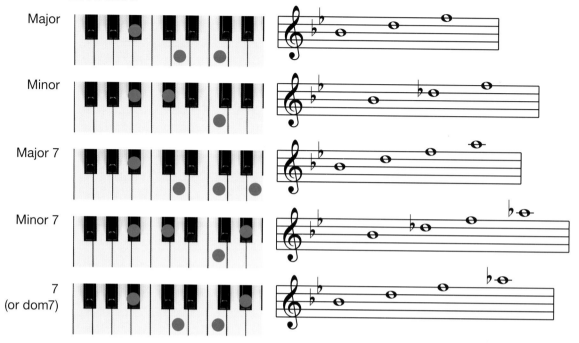

Major

Minor

Major 7

Minor 7

7
(or dom7)

B Chords

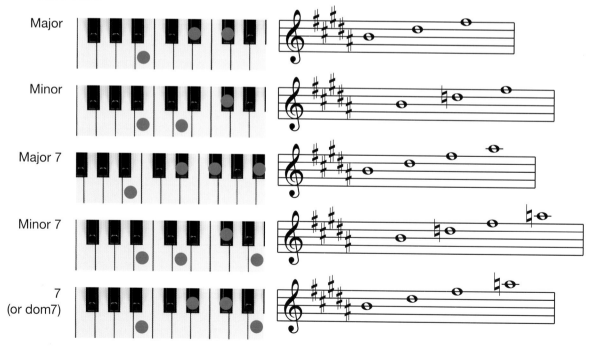

Major

Minor

Major 7

Minor 7

7
(or dom7)

RULES FOR CHORD PROGRESSIONS

Some chords are more important because they have specific duties.

THE 1 CHORD

The 1 chord is also known as the **tonic** or **root** chord and it is the most important because this is 'home'.

If you play a tune starting on C, play a couple of other chords and finish back at C, it all feels complete. If you land on another chord, it will feel unfinished.

THE 5 CHORD

The next most important chord is the 5 chord. It always wants to 'go home'; that is, it pulls, or leads, towards the 1 (root/tonic) chord. For example, G7 always wants to go to C, not Em or F. It is all about how much 'pull' or tension the chord has.

THE 4 CHORD

The next most important chord is the 4 chord. It doesn't have as strong a pull as 5. For example, F–C it pulls a bit, but not as much as G–C. F–C is gentler. (The 4–1 progression is often used in the 'A-men' at the end of traditional church music.)

OTHER CHORDS

The remaining chords basically have equal standing. Try it for yourself: play G7 to C and get used to the sound.

Now play Dm, Am, Em, B dim. They don't feel like they want to go anywhere in particular (although you'll find that they have their own tensions and releases when you become more familiar with them).

The 2–5–1 progression is particularly strong. By playing the 2 before the 5, it is in a way becoming a 5–1 of its own. D going down to G is a 5–1 in the scale of G.

Why do you need to know this? It helps to understand what the harmony (the progression of chords) is doing.

Don't worry if this is confusing for now. It will become clear as you play with it. It is important to understand and recognise tension and release in music if you wish to compose music. If there is no tension and release, music sounds unmoving and bland: a bit the same as a painting without any contrast.

IMPROVISATION: SCALES

One of the exciting things about the piano is improvising (or playing 'off the top of your head'). Of course, it can be done on any instrument, however on the piano you can accompany yourself while you do it.

There are many styles in which you can improvise. Make sure you are familiar with the common major and minor chords before you start. There are three more scales that are important to know and, armed with these, you'll be able to play most styles, from rock to jazz to country.

MINOR SCALES

C MAJOR TO A NATURAL MINOR

Play the scale of C major and look at the keys. Now, find the sixth degree: A.

If you now play the scale of C major starting on A, you are playing another scale known as A natural minor.

There are many types of minor scales. Scales become minor because their third degree is lowered by a semitone, which is the same thing you do to create a minor chord. The other notes in a scale can be raised or lowered to form different types of minor scales, but it is the lowered third that determines whether a scale is actually major or minor.

G MAJOR TO E NATURAL MINOR

Do the same with the G major scale. Play it and look at the keys.

Start on its sixth degree, and you will play an E natural minor scale.

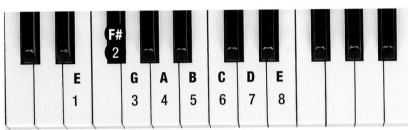

When you create a minor scale in this way, you are creating what's known as the **relative minor** to the major scale you started with. So, A minor is the relative minor scale to C major, E minor is the relative minor scale to G major and so on.

Take some time to learn these scales to begin with – naturally you will want to know all 12 major and minor scales, but these are popular and easy to learn for now.

Major scale: **C**, **G**, **D**, **A**, **F**   Minor scale: **A**, **E**, **G**, **C**, **D**

The next two types of scale (pentatonic and blues) will probably be the most useful scales for basic improvisation.

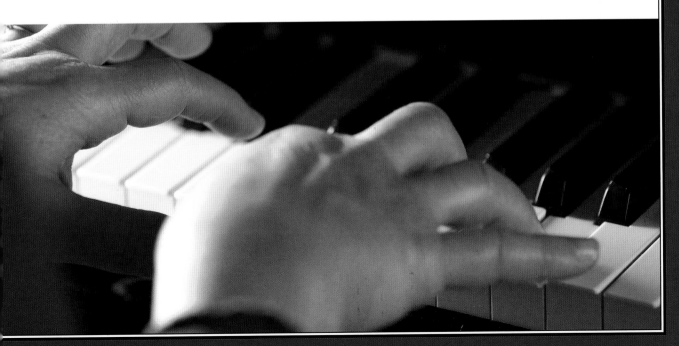

PENTATONIC SCALE

A pentatonic scale only has five notes in it. To create a pentatonic scale, take a major scale and remove the 4th and 7th degrees. To play a pentatonic scale in C, you would play:

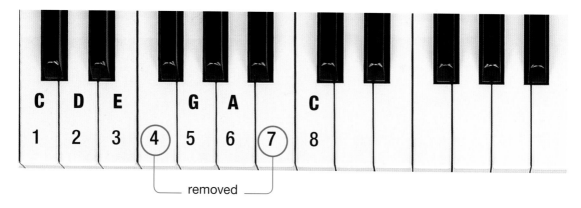

The pentatonic scale is a major-sounding scale, so it's great to use it when you want to improvise a melody over a major chord. It sounds nicer than playing a normal major scale over a major chord because it has intervals built into it, whereas the major scale is one note after another. (An **interval** is the space from one note to the next.) Playing just the black keys also creates a pentatonic scale.

Listen to the piece *Morning* from *Pier Gynt* for a good example of how pretty the pentatonic scale can sound in a melody.

If you have a major-sounding chord progression, you can use the pentatonic scale to improvise a melody. Notice how all of these chords belong to the scale of C major.

BLUES SCALE

The blues scale occurs in the same way as a minor scale – it is the relative minor scale to the pentatonic scale, but with a slight twist. Like a minor scale, it has the third lowered by a semitone.

Start on C and play the C pentatonic scale.

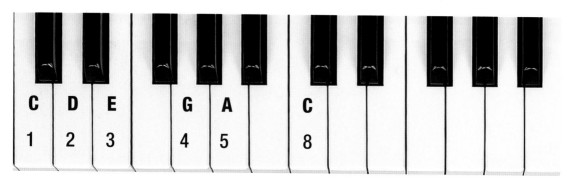

Start on the sixth degree, which in this case is A. This creates an A minor pentatonic scale.

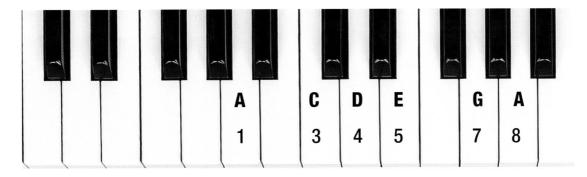

Now add another note after the fourth degree: in this case, D#. This creates an A blues scale.

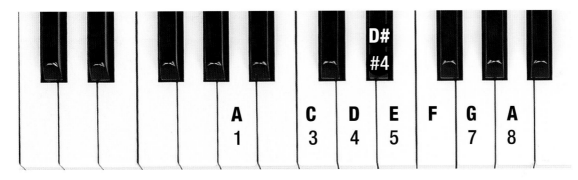

Good choices of intervals with tension and release in a melody create a great piece of improvised music. Some good examples of this include the classic song *Somewhere Over the Rainbow* and the Beatles song *Yesterday*.

IMPROVISATION: CHORDS AND MELODIES

Improvisation is something that you do by 'ear'. You don't use any written music apart from maybe a few chords that you use to improvise a melody over. Jazz musicians often do this.

IMPROVISING IN THE KEY OF C

An easy way to start improvisation is to begin in the key of C major, and use two of its chords: C and G (the 1 and 5 chords).

Begin by counting in at a comfortable tempo. Play the C chord for one bar, then the G chord for one bar and keep repeating this.

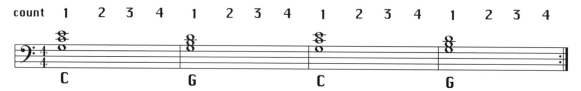

As these two chords belong to the scale of C major, technically any note from that scale should work as a melody. You'll find that some work better than others.

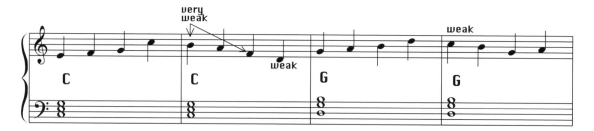

This is where listening to the notes you choose is important. Decide whether you have made a good note choice for the chord. Some notes work better than others over certain chords. When improvising, however, remember that there is no right or wrong; it's up to you because you are the 'composer'.

IMPROVISING IN OTHER KEYS

Once you're comfortable with this, try improvising in other keys. For example:
• In the scale of G major, the 1 and 5 chords are G and D.
• In F major, the 1 and 5 chords are F and C.
• In D major, the 1 and 5 chords are D and A.

You may have to think about it the first few times you play, but you will soon remember the 1 and 5 chords of the different scales and improvising will start to feel easier.

Another helpful tool when learning to improvise a melody is to first sing one in your head or out loud and then try to play it. This is also a great way of training your ear to hear and then play. It's a very useful musical skill.

As you do this, think about where the melody moves up or down. For instance, take the melody to *Three Blind Mice*. Think about where it goes up and down and then try to play it. Try this with other well-known melodies to fast track your ear training.

THE 12 BAR BLUES

One of the most popular chord progressions is the 12 bar blues, which, in its basic form, uses the 1, 4 and 5 chords of the major scale. It is used in many different musical styles; rock, jazz, blues, country, piano boogie to name a few.

This 12 bar chord pattern is repeated over and over.

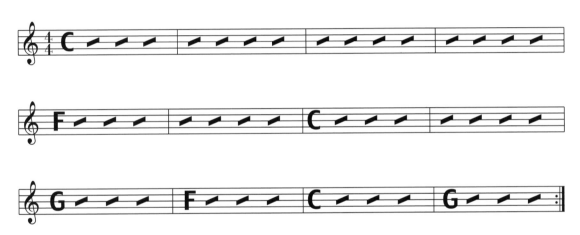

Most of these examples are done in C. This is standard practice but it is assumed that you will transpose the example to a key that suits you (or you can stay in C – some of life's great musicians have only written in C!). A funny thing about the blues scale is that it is neither major nor minor, and that's one of the things that make it so versatile.

To try improvising, choose one of the scales and apply different rhythms to it. Create patterns that repeat at different places in the scale. Don't be afraid to play a 'hole'; that is, leave spaces occasionally so it's not crowded with notes. Remember to try singing parts of a melody before playing it.

When you're comfortable with a bit of improvisation, try working with more than one scale. Use the pentatonic and blues scales in the one piece and then use some of the major scale. A very rough guideline is that you can use a major or pentatonic scale over a major chord and a minor or blues scale over a minor chord.

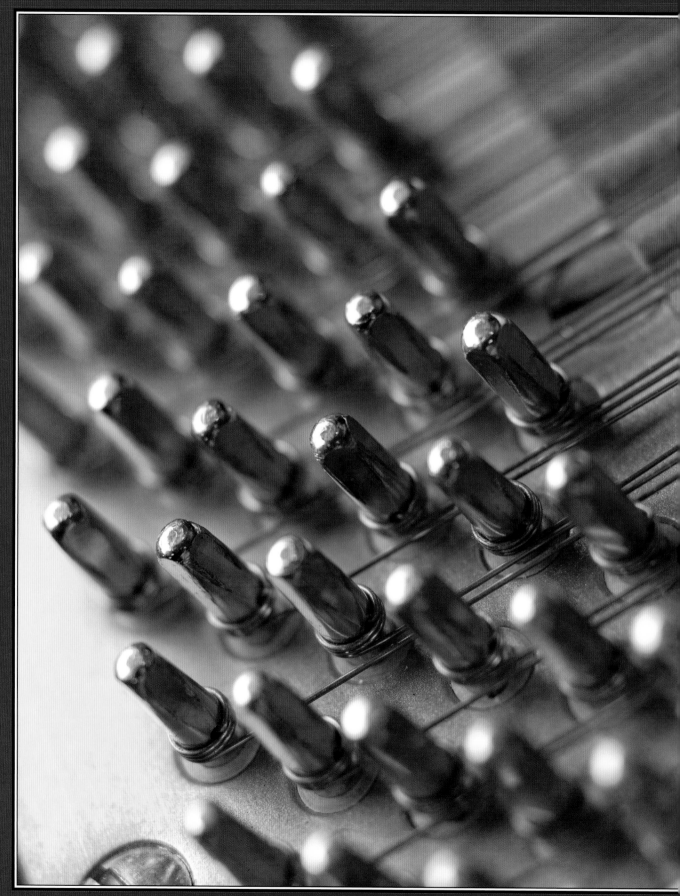

TWO NEW CHORDS

These last two chords are the diminished and the augmented chords. The shorthand when writing them is:
• dim or ° (for example, C dim or C°)
• aug or + (for example, C aug or C+).
These chords have a tremendous amount of pull to them.

DIMINISHED CHORDS

To make a C diminished chord, take the C major chord and flatten the third (as you do to make a minor chord), but also flatten the fifth. The notes in the chord are C, E♭ and G♭. Try this along with other chords.

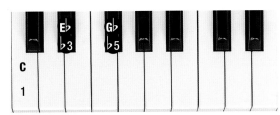

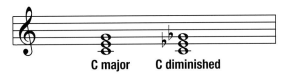

Play these chord progressions and listen to how they sound.

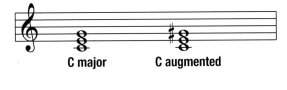

| C   C dim ‖ | G   G dim ‖ |

AUGMENTED CHORDS

To make a C augmented chord, take the C major chord and sharpen the fifth. The notes in the chord are C, E and G#. Again, try this along with other chords.

Play this chord progression and listen to how it sounds.

| 4/4 C   C + | F | F   F + | G   G + | C   ‖ |

CONCLUSION

I hope that after working your way through *Simply Piano*, you have a greater insight into music itself, as well as the piano and keyboard instruments. I encourage you to regularly spend time with the piano, either practising, listening to your favourite music and trying to play it on the piano, or just amusing yourself with the sound of different chords played in succession and working out melodies to fit over them.

Use the internet to watch pianists and try to follow what they are doing. Get together with other piano players and talk piano with them. Even consider teaching someone how to play, no matter how little you think you know. There's always something you can pass on and it reinforces your knowledge. Take occasional lessons from any teacher who is happy to teach on a casual basis – they may provide you with ideas that can take weeks to work through at your own pace.

If you can, play a little every day. You'll be amazed at how well you progress if you play as little as 15 minutes every day (time flies when you practise the piano and you'll often play for longer than you set out to). A little every day is far more beneficial than one large chunk every so often.

More than anything, I hope it was a joy for you to work through *Simply Piano* and that it has enhanced your piano playing pleasure.

ABOUT THE AUTHOR

Robyn Payne is a composer, arranger and music producer for albums and TV and radio jingles.

Robyn began playing piano at six years old after her parents tired of her banging out a tune on anything she could find, especially a toy xylophone. After a few years of piano lessons, she took up guitar, playing solo and with bands. Looking for more musical challenges, she joined a brass band to learn trumpet and discovered a love of the bass. In her final year at school, Robyn learnt flute and played in the school orchestra. At college, it was recommended that she do a woodwind major alongside piano and bass, so she studied clarinet and saxophone.

After graduating with a Bachelor of Education in music, Robyn found herself in many bands, in demand as a pianist and a multi-keyboard player. Years of playing and recording with many bands and artists followed, along with a second music degree, in classical piano.

Robyn has played as a backing artist for many performers, including Tom Jones, Joe Cocker, Barry Manilow, BB King, Bonnie Raitt, Jackson Browne, Larry Adler and Marina Prior, to name a few. She has toured with artists such as Tommy Emmanuel, Tina Arena and The Seekers. Robyn also played in the band for the long-running Australian television program *Hey Hey It's Saturday* for six years and wrote the opening theme for the show.

In 2001, Robyn was a guest lecturer at the School of Creative Arts in Singapore. She currently sits on the industry advisory panel for the Northern Metropolitan College of TAFE in Melbourne and is an examiner for mid- and end-of-year recitals at the TAFE.